Day 8

Worship Art

First edition

2023

Book Name: Day 8

The Author: *Worship Art*

Translated by: Fady Guirguis

Translation checking: M. Magdy
Cover design: Kerols Fouad

First edition 2023

Deposit number: 26572/ 2022
ISBN : 978-977-321-355-8

Publisher: *Worship Art*
For communication:

USA WhatsApp: +17187577428
WhatsApp/ Telegram: (+2) 01277577697
E-mail: worshipart@yahoo.com
Facebook: @worshipartkingdom
Instagram: worshipart.abc
YouTube (Arabic channel): @worshipart2885

Table of Contents

Introduction

Have you ever questioned why the modern-day church looks very different than the early day church [church of the apostles]? And why despite this being the age of grace, do we still have an Old Testament approach to life and often even marvel at Old Testament experiences and wish to experience if not some of it ourselves?

Have you come across this verse before?

"And the Lord gave them rest all around"- 2 Chr 15:15

Is it just another verse you read and let it pass by? Have you stood before the Lord and asked him to give you that life of rest?

We all want to rest that is for sure, yet we don't understand the kind of rest that is offered to us, and more importantly how to enter into it and be settled there.

I invite you to still your heart for a moment and quiet the tempest that often rages in the form of memories, day to day thoughts and experiences, all with the sole purpose of uprooting you from this very truth of "rest".

I ask the Lord to open the eyes of your understanding because I believe the Holy Spirit would like you to possess the truth of what it means to 'dwell in rest all around' for why would the Holy Spirit mention such a truth if it was not an invitation for you and me to live it?

My prayer is that you find revelation light in the words I am about to write and share with you and this light will shine bright into any dark places and areas of your life keeping you from experiencing the fullness of living in the rest that has been offered to you.

"And on the seventh day God ended His work which He had done, and He rested on the seventh day from all His work which He had done."- Gen 2: 2

"For this reason, the Jews persecuted Jesus and sought to kill Him, because He had done these things on the Sabbath. But Jesus answered them, "My Father has been working until now, and I have been working."- John 5: 16-17

The question that comes to mind after reading these verses is: Has God rested from all his work or is He still working?

It is mentioned in Genesis that on the seventh day the Lord rested from all his work, but that rest did not last as intended. For with the fall of man, God, came out of his rest, as did man, and God went back to "working" to create a new kind of rest for man that the enemy can't influence, corrupt or steal ever again. **For "The Sabbath was made for man, and not man for the Sabbath"- Mark 2: 27**

Have these words shocked you? Great, let us dive deeper into the revelation of salvation, which is way more than just the forgiveness of sins.

In the beginning, the Lord created man to reign and subdue creation [via the authority that came from being in communal relationship with him]. But the serpent corrupted all that the Lord created and deemed 'good' by corrupting man's MIND, that is why "the renewing of our minds" is a key to unlocking mysteries and revelations that in turn transform our lives.

Amidst all this corruption and through the judgments the Lord spoke over man, the earth and the serpent, the Lord made a way out when he prophesied over Eve and said:

"And between your seed and her Seed, He shall bruise/crush your head [The serpent]"- Gen 3: 15

In speaking these words, he put an end to the serpent's corrupt authority [one of the very first prophecies that spoke of his redemption].

And for years the Lord has been preparing for this day, THE day, when all creation will be set free from the corruption that was caused by the fall in the beginning.

I can understand if your mind is struggling or even rejecting what I just wrote and rightly so, but please allow me to demonstrate to you that this is based on biblical truth.

"Therefore, since a promise remains of entering His rest, let us fear lest any of you seem to have come short of it. For indeed the gospel was preached to us as well as to them; but the word which they heard did not profit them, not being mixed with faith in those who heard it. For we who have believed do enter that rest, as He has said: "So, I swore in My wrath, they shall not enter My rest". Although the works were finished from the foundation of the

world. For He has spoken in a certain place of the seventh day in this way: "And God rested on the seventh day from all His works" and again in this place: "They shall not enter My rest." Since therefore it remains that some must enter it, and those to whom it was first preached did not enter because of disobedience, again He designates a certain day, saying in David, "Today" after such a long time, as it has been said: "Today, if you will hear His voice, do not harden your hearts."

For if Joshua had given them rest, then He would not afterward have spoken of another day. There remains therefore a rest for the people of God. For he who has entered His rest has himself also ceased from his works as God did from His. Let us therefore be diligent to enter that rest, lest anyone fall according to the same example of disobedience." - Heb 4: 1-11

Did you notice how the bible spoke about 'a certain day' that is not of the original seven days?

YES!

'There remains therefore a rest for the people of God' constant and never changing: This certain 'new day' that the bible calls the Eighth Day.

For many years we, the church, have lost sight of this truth and of the revelation it carries and ended up living lives so distant and very different to the lives of the apostles and the early church, lacking in power and glory, while they [the apostles] remained steadfast despite all the trials and tribulations, why is that? Because they dwelt and lived their lives in the fullness of this truth, they believed that this day of rest contained and released power that was much stronger than anything they would face. In fact, I believe it was the key that unlocked all the marvelous things they did, lived, experienced leaving us in awe as we read about them in the bible.

What is the Eighth Day?

The most common and spontaneous answer I hear is: "The Eighth day is eternity."

I am aware this answer is correct 100% but my question is this: Does eternity only mean your life in heaven after you've been resurrected?

If your answer to this question is yes, then allow us to go over a few verses of scripture together:

"He has made everything beautiful in its time. Also, He has put eternity in their hearts, except that no one can find out the work that God does from beginning to end" Eccl 3: 11

"Now when He was asked by the Pharisees when the kingdom of God would come, He answered them and said, "The kingdom of God does not come with observation nor will they say, 'See here!' or 'See there!' For indeed, the kingdom of God is within you" Luke 17: 20-21

You are aware that your spirit man is eternal and since He, the spirit, is within you and is also eternal, therefore eternity and the kingdom forever dwell within you. Thus, we aren't only talking about life after departing this earthly body but about the reality of where your spirit man currently dwells and abides.

Therefore, the Eighth Day is eternity within you here on earth, today, that also continues with you till the day you remove this earthly tent that is your body.

When was the Eighth Day Designated?

Before we determine when the Eighth Day began, let us not forget that from the Lord's perspective, it is not measured in hours as we do here on earth, let us go back to the beginning, to Genesis, to read and see how a day ended and how every new day began.

There are certain phrases the Lord used to end a day's work [for example: **"And there was evening, and there was morning", "And God saw that", "it was good."**

That is why the Lord had to end the seventh day to usher in a new day**, the day he designated**, **the eighth day** the day where all his people can enter and find rest just like he did.

Thus, The Lord through divine inspiration used a very specific expression called; "the fullness of time" in referring to the day of his birth: **"Even so we, when we were children, were in bondage under the elements of the world. But when the fullness of the time had come, God sent forth His Son, born of a woman, born under the law, to redeem those who were under the law, that we might receive the adoption as sons. And because you are sons, God has sent forth the Spirit of His Son into your hearts, crying out, "Abba, Father!" Therefore, you are no longer a slave but a son, and if a son, then an heir of God through Christ." – Gal 4: 3-7**

So, what is the fullness of time? It is the exact and acceptable time that the Lord saw in his eternal wisdom, to put an end to the seventh day and usher in the beginning of a new day, the eighth day. And as we know from the book of Genesis to each day were assigned specific tasks to be done/completed on the day, yet when it came to the eighth day, the allotment of this new day [the eighth day] wasn't just purposed for his birth. His birth was just the start, for we find the spirit repeating the same phrase: **"Having made known to us the mystery of His will, according to His good pleasure which He purposed in Himself, <u>that in the dispensation of the fullness of the times He might gather together in one all things in Christ, both which are in heaven and which are on earth—in Him</u>. In Him also we have obtained an inheritance, being predestined according to the purpose of Him who works all things according to the counsel of His will, that we who first trusted in Christ should be to the praise of His glory. In Him you also trusted, after you heard the word of truth, the gospel of your salvation; in whom also, having believed, you were sealed with the Holy Spirit of promise, who is the guarantee of our inheritance until the redemption of the purchased possession, to the praise of His glory" - Eph 1: 9-14**

From the previous verses, the Holy Spirit tells us that there is a secret behind the change that occurred in the fullness of time. There was a purpose in the Lord's soul, and that the dispensation of the fullness of time is what explains to us the secret of the Father's will, and this secret is summed up in two words: reconciliation and adoption.

As he tells us through his words to the Galatians, redemption was not just about getting rid of the penalty for our sins, as some think, but also about receiving adoption, so we transition from slaves to sons who have the right to inherit.

Then he goes on further to explain the matter in his letter to the Ephesians, assuring us that the plan for the dispensation of the fullness of time has a purpose and will. It is a goal that the Lord intended to reach from the beginning, and this purpose is represented in the reconciliation of those who accept the word of truth and the work of redemption.

This reconciliation cancels the deed of bondage off our lives and seals for us our new birth certificate with the Holy Spirit, making it clear that this seal in reality is nothing but a pledge/down payment of the inheritance for which the Son redeemed us.

The Lord did not erase this deed of bondage from specific people, as if he was a slave master showing mercy to his slaves, because humanity was not enslaved to the Lord, but rather to death.

The Lord intended to completely eradicate the legality of the deed. That is why God had to eradicate the entire slavery system along with all of its law. This necessitated changing entire times by crushing and defeating death and stripping it of the sovereignty it had over all humanity keeping us enslaved so that we could have absolute freedom to choose. Either we live in previous times under the bondage of death, despite the work of the Son, or we enter into the Lord's rest and enjoy what He has provided for us in the fullness of time.

The Lord put an end to the seventh day here to usher in the new day and described it by saying it required a special dispensation. This was not just another day on earth, NO, this was a start of a new age, a day the spirit prophetically spoke of when saying: **"This is the day**

the Lord has made; we will rejoice and be glad in it" - Ps 118:24

If you read this Psalm carefully, you will notice that it talks about the sacrifice of the cross. Have you ever questioned why there was darkness (Evening) while Jesus was being crucified? And why did he give up his spirit as the day was ending and a new day was on the horizon?

Reading the previous verse, we can see that the Lord had indeed created a new day, The Eighth Day via Redemption through the work done on the cross and resurrection. And so, it started out with the evening of the Eighth Day, even though we only had access to dwell and live in it, after it was sealed the day, the Holy Spirit was poured out on Pentecost. This is because the matter did not end with the resurrection, but rather with the ascension of the Son and with him the ascension of all who believe in order to change their place of residence from Earth, subject to the darkness of this age, to obtaining the legality of dwelling in the light of the Father's face.

"But God, who is rich in mercy, because of His great love with which He loved us, even when we were dead in trespasses, made us alive together with Christ (by grace you have been saved), and raised us up together, <u>and made us sit together in the heavenly places</u> in Christ Jesus, <u>that in the ages to come He might show the exceeding riches of His grace</u> in His kindness toward us in Christ Jesus." - Eph 2: 4-7

The Father showed us the riches of His mercy, grace, and kindness in what He did for us in Christ Jesus, when He saved us from the penalty of our sins, which is death, and raised us up in Christ, and seated us with Him in the heavenly places.

You have to believe this! You and I and everyone who believes in Him will no longer abide under the judgment of the fall that occurred on the seventh day.

Notice what Jesus said on the cross: **"So, when Jesus had received the sour wine, He said, "It is finished!"' –John 19: 30**

To whom did Jesus speak these words and why?

Jesus was not on earth just to redeem us from our sins. He was also redeeming that day of rest. The day He originally created for us to live in complete communion with him. The day that was corrupted due to the fall. The day we were no longer able to have access and enter into.

The Holy Spirit used the same word used in the book of Genesis: **"Thus the heavens and the earth, and all the host of them, were finished." - Gen 2:1**

Yes! This is what happened, as it was at the beginning of creation, Jesus said "it is finished [completed]" he had finished, and to perfection, that which he had originally planned (put an end to the seventh day and create a new day), He restored our ability and our access back into that perfect day, into his rest, the Eighth Day.

"**It is finished**" was spoken by Jesus to and into the spiritual realm, declaring in the same manner as He did back in Genesis, that all that had happened on the seventh day, the fall and life as we knew it from that perspective had ended and a new day begun.

In the Evening (which is when a new day begins, while it is still dark), on the Eighth Day, Jesus descended into the lower earthly realms, disarming the powers, principalities and authorities to abolish the legality of his enslavement of mankind. Then He raised us with Him in His resurrection, and also raised us with Him from the corruption of the fall and sealed the path of our ascension with the Holy Spirit.

The Lord completed the dispensation of the fullness of time by completing reconciliation. This is what the Holy Spirit tells us in the Gospel of John when he wrote Jesus' last conversation with the Father before the journey of the cross, which was the final report of his work on earth: **"Jesus spoke these words, lifted up HIs eyes to heaven, and said: "Father, the hour has come. Glorify Your Son, that Your Son also may glorify You, as You have given Him authority over all flesh, that He should give eternal life to as many as You have given Him. And this is eternal life that they may know you, the only true God, and Jesus Christ whom you have sent. I have glorified you on the earth. I have finished the work which you have given me to do. And now, O Father, glorify me together [b]with yourself, with the glory which I had with you before the world was. "I have manifested your name to the men whom you have given Me out of the world. They**

were Yours, you gave them to me, and they have kept your word. Now they have known that all things which you have given me are from you" – John 7: 1-7

The Spirit was telling us that the purpose of Jesus' ministry on earth was to know the Father. That is why he did not come directly to the cross. He lived under the law and perfected it. Then he went out to serve to tell us about the Father and his kingdom, and this is the secret behind Jesus repeating these words: **"The kingdom of God has come upon you!" - Matt 12:28**

Jesus was explaining in a practical way what the kingdom is and that its true power surpasses any other powers. It brought down Satan like lightning from heaven. The crowds can now hear the voice of the Father directly without the need for a prophet or the high priest who appeared once before the Lord after offering up many sacrifices.

The dispensation of the eighth day changed everything! It opened the way to the Father again, not only to hear from him as servants/slaves asking about the will of their master, but to have the right to sit with him as Sons. And on Pentecost the Holy Spirit sealed within us this new truth, a down payment of the inheritance we receive as we enter the door to the eighth day. If this is the down payment, then what is the full inheritance that we will get if we actually enter and abide with Him in the heavenly places?

Features of the Eighth Day

Have you read what the psalmist said?

"This is the day the Lord has made; we will rejoice and be glad in it." - Ps 118:24

It is clear that we are to Rejoice and be Glad for 'this day' that the Lord created for us.

Rejoicing and being Glad are features of this Eighth Day, they are part of the nature of this day as they are also part of the nature of eternity that dwells within you. All we have to do is live according to this nature residing within us and live what we were created for. And that explains the joy the Early church experienced in the midst of persecution and tribulation.

Let us now move on and study what the spirit tells us in the bible about our identity on this day and live up to its fullness.

Circumcision:

"He who is eight days old among you shall be circumcised, every male child in your generations, he who is born in your house or bought with money from any foreigner who is not your descendant"- Gen 17: 12

The first mention of the Eighth Day was when the Lord commanded Abraham to circumcise every male of his household and the first on whom the commandment was carried out upon was Isaac. Everyone else in Abraham's household, including Ishmael and Abraham himself, was circumcised before Isaac but not on the eighth day.

"Then Abraham circumcised his son Isaac when he was eight days old, as God had commanded him" - Gen 21: 4

For it was a sign that this people have been set apart from the rest of the nations unto the Lord.

If you believe that you are a son and heir and that you are his offspring, then of course you have entered the Eighth Day.

"Now, therefore, you are no longer strangers and foreigners, but fellow citizens with the saints and members of the household of God" - Eph 2: 19

"But he is a Jew who is one inwardly; and circumcision is that of the heart, in the Spirit, not in the letter; whose praise is not from men but from God" - Rom 2: 29

"And you are complete in Him, who is the head of all principality and power. In Him you were also circumcised with the circumcision made without hands, by putting off the body of the sins of the flesh, by the circumcision of Christ" - Col 2: 10-11

Functions of the Eighth Day

1. The Firstborn:

"Likewise, you shall do with your oxen and your sheep. It shall be with its mother seven days; on the eighth day you shall give it to Me" - Exod 22: 30

Every Firstborn that is to be set apart for the Lord must first remain for seven days with his mother before he is presented unto the Lord on the eighth day.

If you believe that we are **"the church of the firstborn" - Heb 12: 23** and that you dwell in that position then you have all the advantages, rights and duties of a Firstborn.

You have indeed been born of the spirit, no longer just born of the flesh thus you have entered the Eighth Day.

2. Priesthood:

"And you shall not go outside the door of the tabernacle of meeting for seven days, until the days of your consecration are ended. For seven days he shall consecrate you. As he has done this day, so the Lord has commanded to do, to make atonement for you. Therefore, you shall stay at the door of the tabernacle of meeting day and night for seven days, and keep the charge of the Lord, so that you may not die; for so I have been commanded." So, Aaron and his sons did all the things that the Lord had commanded by the hand of Moses" - Lev 8: 33-36

"It came to pass on the eighth day that Moses called Aaron and his sons and the elders of Israel. And he said to Aaron, "Take for yourself a young bull as a sin offering and a ram as a burnt offering, without blemish, and offer them before the Lord. And to the children of Israel you shall speak, saying, 'Take a kid of the goats as a sin offering, and a calf and a lamb, both of the first year, without blemish, as a burnt offering, also a bull and a ram as peace offerings, to sacrifice before the Lord, and a grain offering mixed

with oil; for today the Lord will appear to you" - Lev 9: 1-4

Do you see now the steps of a Priests' consecration? They spend seven full days of consecration so that on the Eighth Day they may begin their priesthood.

Let me tell you something important. The sacrifices you offer up from: thanksgiving, praise, generosity, fasting, prostration and any other, vary in its effect according to how aware you are of the nature of your spiritual function, selah!

If you believe that **"you are a chosen people, a royal priesthood" - 1Pet 2: 9** then you are standing in your priestly position on the eighth day before the one who called you.

3. Anointing and Consecrating the Altar:

"And you shall take the anointing oil and anoint the tabernacle and all that is in it; and you shall hallow it and all its utensils, and it shall be holy. You shall anoint the altar of the burnt offering and all its utensils and consecrate the altar. The altar shall be most holy. And you shall anoint the laver and its base, and consecrate it" - Exod 40: 9-11

"Every day for seven days you shall prepare a goat for a sin offering; they shall also prepare a young bull and a ram from the flock, both without blemish. Seven days they shall make atonement for the altar and purify it, and so consecrate it. When these days are over it shall be, on the eighth day and thereafter, that the priests shall offer your burnt offerings and

your peace offerings on the altar; and I will accept you,' says the Lord God" - Ezek 43: 25-27

The book of Exodus doesn't mention the details of setting up the tabernacle nor the details of the consecration of the altar, it also does not mention the details of consecrating the priests, but Ezekiel 43 tells us about the necessary steps. Seven days were needed to make atonement and cleansing and that only on the **Eighth Day** were they able to present acceptable offerings to the Lord on that alter.

If you insist on living your life from the seventh day, know that you are only living in a closed loop of trying to constantly consecrate yourself! and so, every sacrifice you offer up will be about you and making yourself clean and it won't be a sacrifice offered up to be pleasing to the Lord.

The difference is huge. All you need is revelation that transfers you from the vicious circles where you constantly need to be cleansed to a priest who stands before the Lord, face to face with the father.

We must ask the Holy Spirit to bring a new revelation to our lives that will move us from this closed loop of constantly trying to sanctify ourselves and into true priesthood [which is an awareness that we stand with our high priest Jesus Christ on a spiritual altar face to face with the father constantly being cleansed].

4. The Law of ceremonial cleansing:

"Then the priest shall command to take for him who is to be cleansed two living and clean birds, cedar wood, scarlet, and hyssop. And the priest shall command that one of the birds be killed in an earthen vessel over running water. As for the living bird, he shall take it, the cedar wood and the scarlet and the hyssop, and dip them and the living bird in the blood of the bird that was killed over the running water. And he shall sprinkle it seven times on him who is to be cleansed from the leprosy, and shall pronounce him clean, and shall let the living bird loose in the open field. He who is to be cleansed shall wash his clothes, shave off all his hair, and wash himself in water, that he may be clean. After that he shall come into the camp and shall stay outside his tent seven days. But on the seventh day he shall shave all the hair off his head and his beard and his eyebrows—all his hair he shall shave off. He shall wash his clothes and wash his body in water, and he shall be clean and on the eighth day he shall take two male lambs without blemish, one ewe lamb of the first year without blemish, three-tenths of an ephah of fine flour mixed with oil as a grain offering, and one log of oil" - Lev 14: 4-10

Leviticus 14 explains ceremonial cleansing and in doing so reiterates that for seven days they are to be cleansed and must remain outside so that on the Eighth Day they may enter back into camp, cleansed and able to enter their tent.

Do you see how precise the Holy Spirit is in telling us about this day and why it is important for us to understand it?

The eighth day is not a new idea, we were all expelled out of Eden on the seventh day. Therefore, without the consecration that came by the death and resurrection of Jesus we could no longer enter to where God is present in order to walk, talk and see his face. We would still be outside the camp going around in circles trying to enter with our own righteousness thinking that by keeping the law and our good deeds we could once again walk, talk and see him face to face forgetting that he has done and finished all the requirements of the law so that we can now simply and boldly enter to be with him where he is as he is, in rest.

5. Activating the prophetic calling:

"So, the Spirit lifted me up and took me away, and I went in bitterness, in the heat of my spirit; but the hand of the Lord was strong upon me. Then I came to the captives at Tel Abib, who dwelt by the River Chebar; and I sat where they sat and remained there astonished among them seven days. Now it came to pass at the end of seven days that the word of the Lord came to me, saying, "Son of man, I have made you a watchman for the house of Israel; therefore, hear a word from My mouth, and give them warning from Me"- Ezek 3: 14-17

Ezekiel was a priest whom the Lord called to prophecy and become a watchman amongst his people. In chapter 2 you read about how the Lord began speaking to him about his calling and giving him words to keep in his heart, to understand, before he is to utter them. The spirit then lifts him and takes him to the place where he is to be released into this calling.

Did you notice that it said: **"Now it came to pass at the end of seven days"?** Meaning on the **Eighth Day**?

For seven days Ezekiel must have felt confused and probably had no insight into the details of this call nor how to complete it.

I remember the first time I received a prophetic word about my calling, and I remember how perplexed I was and felt at the time, I went and asked the person that spoke the word if he was sure of the words, he had spoken to me saying: "are you sure the Lord spoke these words about ME!? He replied by saying "The voice was too clear for me to doubt it" I looked at him in astonishment and said, "this is strange, for I am far from these words".

Let me tell you, and maybe some of you have experienced what I am about to say, that today, after so many years of receiving those words, I can see them being fulfilled. Day by day being released from strength to strength and from glory to glory.

You could be in the preparation stages, feeling lost, confused, wondering how to take what the Lord has placed in your heart and make it come to pass, but let me tell you that once the seventh day is over, he will give you the understanding you need and release you into the fullness of this calling.

Those little glimpses, the bits and pieces you received over the years were like a down payment to whet your appetite for what is to come, very similar to what happened when Moses asked the spies to bring back some of the fruit from the promise land to whet the peoples' appetite and to unite their hearts to possess the promise land.

So, Today, **"Do not harden your heart"** like they did but **"make every effort to enter into that rest".**

6. Feasts of the Harvest and the Last Day:

Have you ever wondered why the Lord appointed feasts? And why did he insist they would be everlasting/never-ending? Why did he choose their specific timings? And the connection between the feasts?

We often lose the power granted to us through the joy associated with these feasts, as they become more about the food we eat and the new clothes we buy. Families gather, kids hear the stories and these feasts become just another event when in truth they there are to bring real and internal transformation to us. But the Holy spirit shows us in scripture that as we look upon the city of our appointed feasts, our tackles are loosened, we are healed, and the forgiveness of our sins is a guarantee: **"Look**

upon Zion, <u>the city of our appointed feasts</u>, your eyes will see Jerusalem, a quiet home, A tabernacle that will not be taken down, not one of its stakes will ever be removed, nor will any of its cords be broken. But there the majestic Lord will be for us a place of broad rivers and streams, in which no galley with oars will sail, nor majestic ships pass by, for the Lord is our Judge, The Lord is our lawgiver, The Lord is our King, He will save us. <u>Your tackle is loosed</u>, they could not strengthen their mast, they could not spread the sail. Then the prey of great plunder is divided, the lame takes the prey. and <u>the inhabitant will not say, "I am sick", the people who dwell in it will be forgiven their iniquity</u>." - Isa 33: 20-24

In truth, one of the reasons we are not able to fully enjoy the power and the joy these feasts offer us is because we do not fully understand their purpose and the links between them. Which is why I would like to take you through a number of passages in the scripture that talk about these feasts and why the Lord appointed them and try to show you the signs the Holy Spirit leaves for us to understand what He is trying to say.

The Feasts:

"These are the feasts of the Lord, holy convocations which you shall proclaim at their appointed times." - Lev 23: 4

A. Passover:

"On the fourteenth day of the first month at twilight is the Lord's Passover. And on the fifteenth day of the same month is the Feast of Unleavened Bread to the Lord; seven days you must eat unleavened bread. On the first day you shall have a holy convocation; you shall do no customary work on it. But you shall offer an offering made by fire to the Lord for seven days. The seventh day shall be a holy convocation; you shall do no customary work on it.' And the Lord spoke to Moses, saying "Speak to the children of Israel, and say to them: 'When you come into the land which I give to you, and reap its harvest, then you shall bring a sheaf of the firstfruits of your harvest to the priest. He shall wave the sheaf before the Lord, to be accepted on your behalf; on the day after the Sabbath the priest shall wave it. And you shall offer on that day, when you wave the sheaf, a male lamb of the first year, without blemish, as a burnt offering to the Lord. Its grain offering shall be two-tenths of an ephah of fine flour mixed with oil, an offering made by fire to the Lord, for a sweet aroma; and its drink offering shall be of wine, one-fourth of a hin. You shall eat neither bread nor parched grain nor fresh grain until the same day that you have brought an offering to your God; it shall be a statute forever throughout your generations in all your dwellings." - Lev 23: 5-14

Passover celebrations begin on the fourteenth day of the first month [Nisan] at twilight. Celebrations last for 7 days thus making a total of Eight days. That is why at the beginning of this book when we asked, when the eighth day was ordained, the answer was: 'The Eighth Day was ordained by Redemption through the work done on the cross and resurrection.'

Celebrating Passover is basically celebrating redemption and the coming out of bondage and slavery. For on the seventh day, when man fell, mankind became enslaved to Satan and thus under the law of death. But Christ, our Passover, died on our behalf to set us free and released us from this bondage by his blood and resurrection.

Our Lord asked that generation in the wilderness to keep these feasts at their appointed times. Yet, right before entering into the promised land to have a life there he added something to this Passover celebration that wasn't there during the wilderness years and that is the **Firstfruits of the harvest.** For during the first month [Nisan] the wheat harvest was collected and the firstfruit was offered to the Lord and at first glance of reading this you might think that there is no connection between the harvest and Passover, but the spirit tells us this [the tiny signs we mentioned earlier that he leaves for us]: **"But now Christ is risen from the dead and has become the firstfruits of those who have fallen asleep. For since by man came death, by Man also came the resurrection of the dead. For as in Adam all die, even so in Christ all shall be made alive. But each one in his own order: Christ the firstfruits, afterward those**

who are Christ's at His coming. Then comes the end, when He delivers the kingdom to God the Father, when He puts an end to all rule and all authority and power" – 1 Cor 15: 20-24

Jesus Christ himself was the sacrificial lamb [Passover] and he became the firstfruit of those who came out from under the law and power of death, that is why you will hear him saying to Mary and Martha when he resurrected Lazarus from the dead: **"I am the resurrection and the life. He who believes in Me, though he may die, he shall live. And whoever lives and believes in Me shall never die. Do you believe this?" - John 11: 25-26**

In truth, I believe that Jesus was speaking about the defeat of the spirit of death and the end of its rule over all mankind that began on the seventh day and in declaring himself as the firstfruit, we can deduce that we had not yet entered with him into the eighth day. But the door was opened to us on Pentecost.

B. Pentecost

"And you shall count for yourselves from the day after the Sabbath, from the day that you brought the sheaf of the wave offering: seven Sabbaths shall be completed. Count fifty days to the day after the seventh Sabbath; then you shall offer a new grain offering to the Lord. You shall bring from your dwellings two wave loaves of two-tenths of an ephah. They shall be of fine flour; they shall be baked with leaven. They are the first fruits to the Lord. And you shall offer with the bread seven lambs of the first year, without blemish, one young bull, and two rams. They shall be as a burnt offering to

the Lord, with their grain offering and their drink offerings, an offering made by fire for a sweet aroma to the Lord. Then you shall sacrifice one kid of the goats as a sin offering, and two male lambs of the first year as a sacrifice of a peace offering. The priest shall wave them with the bread of the firstfruits as a wave offering before the Lord, with the two lambs. They shall be holy to the Lord for the priest. And you shall proclaim on the same day that it is a holy convocation to you. You shall do no customary work on it. It shall be a statute forever in all your dwellings throughout your generations. When you reap the harvest of your land, you shall not wholly reap the corners of your field when you reap, nor shall you gather any gleaning from your harvest. You shall leave them for the poor and for the stranger: I am the Lord your God" – Lev 23: 15-22

After celebrating Passover and offering the firstfruit of the harvest [the sheaf of the wave offering], count fifty days to celebrate the Harvest [new grain offering] seven sabbaths shall be completed [from Passover] and on the eighth day of the seventh week celebrations for Pentecost [new grain offering] begin, this is the day the Holy Spirit was given for us to receive power to enter the eighth day: **"Having made known to us the mystery of His will, according to His good pleasure which He purposed in Himself, <u>that in the dispensation of the fullness of the times</u> He might gather together in one all things in Christ, both which are in heaven and which are on earth—in Him. In Him also we have obtained an inheritance, being predestined according to the purpose of Him who works all things according to the counsel of His will, that we who first trusted in Christ should be to the praise of His glory. In Him**

you also trusted, after you heard the word of truth, the gospel of your salvation; in whom also, having believed, you were sealed with the Holy Spirit of promise, who is the guarantee of our inheritance until the redemption of the purchased possession, to the praise of His glory." - Eph 1: 9-14

The Holy Spirit is very precise with the words that he uses, He describes the reconciliation of heaven and earth in connection with Pentecost: 'the dispensation of the fullness of times.

This phrase must have stopped you when the spirit used it to describe the birth of our Lord: **"Even so we, when we were children, were in bondage under the elements of the world. But when the fullness of the time had come, God sent forth His Son, born of a woman, born under the law, to redeem those who were under the law, that we might receive the adoption as sons. And because you are sons, God has sent forth the Spirit of His Son into your hearts, crying out, "Abba, Father!" Therefore, you are no longer a slave but a son, and if a son, then an heir of God through Christ." -Gal 4: 3-7**

According to Genesis, specific tasks were ordained for each day, and so in Ephesians it is explained to us that the dispensation of the fullness of times has come, and we must enter this new day, where we receive our salvation and are sealed with the Holy Spirit of promise, who is the guarantee of our inheritance. Then Galatians further expands and tells us that redemption has made us sons, thus, heirs of God through Christ by sending forth the spirit of his Son.

In **John 2**, John tells us that Jesus spoke of the glory of resurrection and the coming of the Holy Spirit all while celebrating the feast of tabernacles and by that linking all the feasts together: **"Now the Jews' Feast of Tabernacles was at hand ""On the last day, that great day of the feast, Jesus stood and cried out, saying, "If anyone thirsts, let him come to Me and drink. He who believes in Me, as the Scripture has said, out of his heart will flow rivers of living water" But this He spoke concerning the Spirit, whom those believing in Him would receive; for the Holy Spirit was not yet given, because Jesus was not yet glorified" – John 7: 2 & 37-39**

So, what then is the feast of the tabernacles?

C. Feast of the Tabernacles (Sukkot)

The feast of the tabernacles is not a commonly celebrated feast in the modern-day church, even though the Lord mandated it an everlasting statute and kept it from generation to generation just like he did with Passover [Easter] and Pentecost. Jesus himself kept these feasts and in their appointed times as well: **"Now the Jews' Feast of Tabernacles was at hand "....... "On the last day, that great day of the feast, Jesus stood and cried out, saying, "If anyone thirsts, let him come to Me and drink. He who believes in Me, as the Scripture has said, out of his heart will flow rivers of living water" But this He spoke concerning the Spirit, whom those believing in Him would receive; for the Holy Spirit was not yet given, because Jesus was not yet glorified" –John 7: 2 & 37-39**

We can clearly see that on the last day of the feast Jesus began speaking to the crowd about the coming outpouring of the Holy Spirit [even though this occurred on Pentecost]. That is why it is important we understand what the feast of tabernacles is to know how it is linked to the outpouring of the Holy Spirit and the last day.

"Speak to the children of Israel, saying: 'The fifteenth day of this seventh month shall be the Feast of Tabernacles for seven days to the Lord. On the first day there shall be a holy convocation. You shall do no customary work on it. For seven days you shall offer an offering made by fire to the Lord. On the eighth day you shall have a holy convocation, and you shall offer an offering made by fire to the Lord. It is a sacred assembly, and you shall do no customary work on it. These are the feasts of the Lord which you shall proclaim to be holy convocations, to offer an offering made by fire to the Lord, a burnt offering and a grain offering, a sacrifice and drink offerings, everything on its day. Besides the Sabbaths of the Lord, besides your gifts, besides all your vows, and besides all your freewill offerings which you give to the Lord. Also, on the fifteenth day of the seventh month, when you have gathered in the fruit of the land, you shall keep the feast of the Lord for seven days; on the first day there shall be a sabbath-rest, and on the eighth day a sabbath-rest. And you shall take for yourselves on the first day the fruit of beautiful trees, branches of palm trees, the boughs of leafy trees, and willows of the brook; and you shall rejoice before the Lord your God for seven days. You shall keep it as a feast to the Lord for seven days in the year. It shall be a statute forever in your generations. You shall celebrate it in the

seventh month. <u>You shall dwell in booths for seven days. All who are native Israelites shall dwell in booths, that your generations may know that I made the children of Israel dwell in booths when I brought them out of the land of Egypt: I am the Lord your God</u>." - Lev 23: 34-43

The feast of the tabernacles is a celebration of **<u>the last harvest</u>** of the year, where they dwelt in booths [or tabernacles, or shelters] as they did after their great exodus and before dwelling in homes in the promised land.

If Passover is symbolic of Christ's redemption, Pentecost is symbolic of the coming of the Holy Spirit, then the feast of tabernacles is symbolic to the life we currently live, dwelling in our earthly bodies. To put it in Paul's words: **"For we know that if our earthly house, this tent [or shelter or tabernacle], is destroyed, we have a building from God, a house not made with hands, eternal in t heavens. For in this we groan, earnestly desiring to be clothed with our habitation which is from heaven, if indeed, having been clothed, we shall not be found naked. For we who are in this tent groan, being burdened, not because we want to be unclothed, but further clothed, that mortality may be swallowed up by life. Now he who has prepared us for this very thing is God, who also has given us the Spirit as a guarantee." - 2 Cor 5: 1-5**

This also explains what Jesus tells us: **"In My Father's house are many mansions; if it were not so, I would have told you. I go to prepare a place for you." John 14: 2**

The life we currently live in these earthly bodies cannot be lived out of our own strength but through the power of the spirit as Paul tells us in **Gal 2: 19-20: "For I through the law died to the law that I might live to God. I have been crucified with Christ; it is no longer I who live, but Christ lives in me; and the life which I now live in the flesh I live by faith in the Son of God, who loved me and gave Himself for me."**

Entering the eighth day is us choosing to die to everything we were before getting to know Christ and being filled with his spirit [born again] giving him full permission to accomplish in us and through us, everything he created us for in the same way Jesus allowed the father to accomplish in him and through him everything he was sent for.

D. The Last Day

Now that we have established biblically how these three feasts are intertwined, allow me to show you how all this is also connected to the last day.

"Then Jesus sent the multitude away and went into the house. And His disciples came to Him, saying, "Explain to us the parable of the tares of the field." He answered and said to them: "He who sows the good seed is the Son of Man. The field is the world, the good seeds are the sons of the kingdom, but the tares are the sons of the wicked one. The enemy who sowed them is the devil, the harvest is the end of the age, and the reapers are the angels. Therefore, as the tares are gathered and burned in the fire, so it will be at the end of this age. The Son of Man will

send out His angels, and they will gather out of His kingdom all things that offend, and those who practice lawlessness, and will cast them into the furnace of fire. There will be wailing and gnashing of teeth. Then the righteous will shine forth as the sun in the kingdom of their Father. He who has ears to hear, let him hear!" - Matt 13: 36-43

Notice here that Jesus interprets the end of the age [or the last day] not as being a day of doom and destruction but of Harvest. This is not just an analogy because he was not narrating the proverb but interpreting it. **Harvest** is the key that links the feasts together with the last day: **"Three times you shall keep a feast to Me in the year: You shall keep the Feast of Unleavened Bread [Passover] you shall, eat unleavened bread seven days, as I commanded you, at the time appointed in the month of Abib, for in it you came out of Egypt; none shall appear before Me empty [firstfruits] and the Feast of Harvest, the firstfruits of your labors which you have sown in the field; and the Feast of Ingathering at the end of the year, when you have gathered in the fruit of your labors from the field. Three times in the year all your males shall appear before the Lord God." - Exod 23: 14-17**

"Speak to the children of Israel and say to them: 'When you come into the land which I give to you, and reap its harvest, then you shall bring a sheaf of the firstfruits of your harvest to the priest. He shall wave the sheaf before the Lord, to be accepted on your behalf; on the day after the Sabbath the priest shall wave it." - Lev 23: 10-11

From these verses we can see the word harvest is obvious and repeated when telling them about Passover

[Firstfruits], the Lord is calling us not to show up before him empty handed but carrying the Firstfruits. Then again when referring to Pentecost: **"And you shall count for yourselves from the day after the Sabbath, from the day that you brought the sheaf of the wave offering: seven Sabbaths shall be completed. Count fifty days to the day after the seventh Sabbath; then you shall offer a new grain offering to the Lord." - Lev 23: 15-16**

and yet again when referring to the feast of the tabernacles [Ingathering of fruit]: **"Also, on the fifteenth day of the seventh month, when you have gathered in the fruit of the land, you shall keep the feast of the Lord for seven days; on the first day there shall be a sabbath-rest, and on the eighth day a sabbath-rest" – Lev 23: 39**

The word harvest is the key word in these verses that links all three feasts [Passover, Pentecost and Tabernacles] and you must notice that this was linked with entering the promised land as there was no harvesting or sowing in the wilderness [manna fell from the sky]: **"Therefore, you shall keep every commandment which I command you today, that you may be strong, and go in and possess the land which you cross over to possess, and that you may prolong your days in the land which the Lord swore to give your fathers, to them and their descendants, 'a land flowing with milk and honey.' For the land which you go to possess is not like the land of Egypt from which you have come, where you sowed your seed and watered it by foot, as a vegetable garden; but the land which you cross over to possess is a land of hills and valleys, which drinks water from the rain of**

heaven, a land for which the Lord your God cares; the eyes of the Lord your God are always on it, from the beginning of the year to the very end of the year. And it shall be that if you earnestly obey My commandments which I command you today, to love the Lord your God and serve Him with all your heart and with all your soul, then I will give you the rain for your land in its season, the early rain and the latter rain, that you may gather in your grain, your new wine, and your oil. And I will send grass in your fields for your livestock, that you may eat and be filled." - Deut 11: 8-15

The curse that was released on the land when Adam fell from Eden has been broken: **"Then to Adam He said, "Because you have heeded the voice of your wife and have eaten from the tree of which I commanded you, saying, 'You shall not eat of it': "Cursed is the ground for your sake, in toil you shall eat of it all the days of your life. Both thorns and thistles it shall bring forth for you, and you shall eat the herb of the field. In the sweat of your face, you shall eat bread till you return to the ground, for out of it you were taken, for dust you are and to dust you shall return." - Gen 3: 17-19**

Yes. The curse has been broken in the city of our God [our promised land]. Now you can harvest a land that drinks its water from the rain of heaven, a safe and constant source. All your needs met and fulfilled as it was in Eden, that is why the Lord made them march seven full days around Jericho and then blow the trumpets before entering the first city of the promised land: **"Now Jericho was securely shut up because of the children of Israel; none went out, and none came**

in. And the Lord said to Joshua: "See! I have given Jericho into your hand, its king, and the mighty men of valor. You shall march around the city, all you men of war; you shall go all around the city once. This you shall do six days. And seven priests shall bear seven trumpets of rams' horns before the ark. But the seventh day you shall march around the city seven times and the priests shall blow the trumpets. It shall come to pass, when they make a long blast with the ram's horn, and when you hear the sound of the trumpet that all the people shall shout with a great shout; then the wall of the city will fall down flat. And the people shall go up every man straight before him." – Josh 6: 1-5

The Holy Spirit confirms that entering the promised land took place after the people were all circumcised, celebrated Passover and eaten from the harvest of the land, then came the trumpet blasts to signify entering the city.

It is as if the Spirit encapsulated all the feasts. In order to see it fully we must revisit what the Lord Jesus said about the signs of his second coming: **"Then the sign of the Son of Man will appear in heaven, and then all the tribes of the earth will mourn, and they will see the Son of Man coming on the clouds of heaven with power and great glory. And He will send His angels with a great sound of a trumpet, and they will gather together His elect from the four winds, from one end of heaven to the other" – Matt 24: 30-31**

He then goes on to say: **"Then the kingdom of heaven shall be likened to ten virgins who took their lamps and went out to meet the bridegroom. Now five of**

them were wise, and five were foolish. Those who were foolish took their lamps and took no oil with them, but the wise took oil in their vessels with their lamps. But while the bridegroom was delayed, they all slumbered and slept. "And at midnight a cry was heard: 'Behold, the bridegroom is coming; go out to meet him!' Then all those virgins arose and trimmed their lamps. And the foolish said to the wise, 'Give us some of your oil, for our lamps are going out.' But the wise answered, saying, 'No, lest there should not be enough for us and you; but go rather to those who sell, and buy for yourselves.' And while they went to buy, the bridegroom came, and those who were ready went in with him to the wedding; and the door was shut. "Afterward the other virgins came also, saying, 'Lord, Lord, open to us!' But he answered and said, 'Assuredly, I say to you, I do not know you. "Watch therefore, for you know neither the day nor the hour in which the Son of Man is coming" – Matt 25: 1-13

That is why you find the Feast of Trumpets and the Day of Atonement before the Feast of Tabernacles: **"Then the Lord spoke to Moses, saying, "Speak to the children of Israel, saying: 'In the seventh month, on the first day of the month, you shall have a sabbath-rest, a memorial of blowing of trumpets, a holy convocation. You shall do no customary work on it; and you shall offer an offering made by fire to the Lord.'" And the Lord spoke to Moses, saying: "Also the tenth day of this seventh month shall be the Day of Atonement. It shall be a holy convocation for you; you shall afflict your souls, and offer an offering made by fire to the Lord. And you shall do no work on that same day, for it is the Day of Atonement, to make atonement for you before the Lord your God. For any person who is not afflicted in soul on that**

same day shall be cut off from his people. And any person who does any work on that same day, that person I will destroy from among his people. You shall do no manner of work; it shall be a statute forever throughout your generations in all your dwellings. It shall be to you a sabbath of solemn rest, and you shall afflict your souls; on the ninth day of the month at evening, from evening to evening, you shall celebrate your sabbath." Then the Lord spoke to Moses, saying, "Speak to the children of Israel, saying: 'The fifteenth day of this seventh month shall be the Feast of Tabernacles for seven days to the Lord. 35 On the first day there shall be a holy convocation. You shall do no customary work on it. 36 For seven days you shall offer an offering made by fire to the Lord. On the eighth day you shall have a holy convocation, and you shall offer an offering made by fire to the Lord. It is a sacred[c] assembly, and you shall do no customary work on it." – Lev 23: 23-36

As you can see, the Holy Spirit kept pointing out signals to us, it starts with circumcision [where we enter into the covenant] then the feast of Passover and harvesting the land then the blowing of the trumpets that alerts the virgins [people of God] to enter into the city of God [the eternal tabernacles]

For long we understood that we are either one or the other from the parable of the foolish and wise virgins but in the parable, we also read about those who cried out at midnight alerting the town that the bridegroom had come reminding me of what Jesus told the disciples: **"And as you go, preach, saying, 'The kingdom of heaven is at hand" – Matt 10: 7**

From the many parables that speak about the kingdom of God, we can deduce that there is more than just being a wise or a foolish virgin, there are those invited to the

wedding, those who help and serve at the wedding, and the friends of the bridegroom [like the disciples and apostles].
You can be one of those invited like the virgins, but you can also be one of the priests carrying a trumpet, crying out 'the bridegroom is coming' to prepare those around you for the wedding, to enter under the cover of his tabernacle in the city of our appointed feasts.
You have now been restored to the way the Lord always intended. You now work the land as caretaker to help provide for those around you, not to meet your needs and personal satisfaction. Jesus has completed and fulfilled the firstfruits of our harvest on the seventh day, to open for us the eighth day with the harvest of the resurrection from the dead, to live and eat from the fruit of his labors, while we sow on the eighth day what the Lord and his angels will reap in the last harvest on the last day.
Yes, Jesus opened for us the gates to the city of our appointed feasts, where the way to the tree of life is: **"Through whom also we have access by faith into this grace in which we stand and rejoice in hope of the glory of God." - Rom 5: 2** and **"Blessed are those who do His commandments, that they may have the right to the tree of life and may enter through the gates into the city." - Rev 22: 14**

It is only in and from this place that we have real authority.

You might think that because these words are written towards the end of the book of revelation then they are talking about a time after we die and have received our new heavenly bodies, but that is not true: **"And he**

showed me a pure river of water of life, clear as crystal, proceeding from the throne of God and of the Lamb. In the middle of its street, and on either side of the river, was the tree of life, which bore twelve fruits, each tree yielding its fruit every month. The leaves of the tree were for the healing of the nations. And there shall be no more curse, but the throne of God and of the Lamb shall be in it, and His servants shall serve Him. They shall see His face, and His name shall be on their foreheads." - Rev 22: 1-4

Do you recall David, describing the righteous as: **"He shall be like a tree planted by the rivers of water, that brings forth its fruit in its season, whose leaf also shall not wither; and whatever he does shall prosper." - Ps 1: 3**

The Holy Spirit in revelation depicts and paints the exact same picture, for if indeed this will all come to pass after we have died and been resurrected, why then is there a need for the leaves of the tree to bring healing to the nations?

There is a path full of life prepped and ready for all the nations on the eighth day.

In the Old Testament, only those who had been circumcised were allowed to partake and celebrate Passover: **"And the Lord said to Moses and Aaron, "This is the ordinance of the Passover: No foreigner shall eat it. But every man's servant who is bought for money, when you have circumcised him, then he may eat it. A sojourner and a hired servant shall not eat it. In one house it shall be eaten, you shall not**

carry any of the flesh outside the house, nor shall you break one of its bones. All the congregation of Israel shall keep it. And when a stranger dwells with you and wants to keep the Passover to the Lord, let all his males be circumcised, and then let him come near and keep it; and he shall be as a native of the land. For no uncircumcised person shall eat it. One law shall be for the native-born and for the stranger who dwells among you." - Exod 12: 43-49

That all changed after Pentecost: **"You shall count seven weeks for yourself; begin to count the seven weeks from the time you begin to put the sickle to the grain. Then you shall keep the Feast of Weeks to the Lord your God with the tribute of a freewill offering from your hand, which you shall give as the Lord your God blesses you. You shall rejoice before the Lord your God, you and your son and your daughter, your male servant and your female servant, the Levite who is within your gates, the stranger and the fatherless and the widow who are among you, at the place where the Lord your God chooses to make His name abide. And you shall remember that you were a slave in Egypt, and you shall be careful to observe these statutes. You shall observe the Feast of Tabernacles seven days, when you have gathered from your threshing floor and from your winepress. And you shall rejoice in your feast, you and your son and your daughter, your male servant and your female servant and the Levite, the stranger and the fatherless and the widow, who are within your gates. Even days you shall keep a sacred feast to the Lord your God in the place which the Lord chooses, because the Lord your God will bless you in all your produce and in all the**

work of your hands, so that you surely rejoice." - Deut 16:9-15

Did you notice how in Exodus [for Passover] only those that were physically circumcised were allowed to partake and celebrate [male circumcision gave permission to the women, slaves, foreigners to be considered circumcised as well] while during the feast of tabernacles as mentioned in Deuteronomy, everyone under the tabernacle of God's people [male and female servants, the stranger, the fatherless, the widow] could partake? it was now open to all, everyone was allowed to celebrate and rejoice in the Lord! All this is made possible because circumcision in the New Testament has changed and is no longer about the physical act but rather one of the hearts: **"Circumcision is that of the heart, in the Spirit, not in the letter; whose praise is not from men but from God." - Rom 2: 29**

Is it clear now what really happened on Pentecost?

The Lord established his heavenly tabernacle here on earth and opened its gates to all who wanted to enter, to all the nations of the earth: **"When they heard these things, they became silent; and they glorified God, saying, "Then God has also granted to the Gentiles repentance to life." - Acts 11: 18**

The Holy Spirit is always very precise when it comes to timings, Passover begins and then on **the eighth day of the seventh week** we come to the feast of tabernacles or [the harvest], for the eighth day is the day of the harvest, harvesting people from every nation, to become sons in the kingdom, and it is specifically this that connects it to the last day [end of the age].

That is why the eighth day functions differently, it does not depend on following a bunch of rules nor keeping certain commandments nor fulfilling certain requirements nor does it depend on your performance [i.e., works], it solely depends on grace: **"Having wiped out the handwriting of requirements that was against us, which was contrary to us. And He has taken it out of the way, having nailed it to the cross. Having disarmed principalities and powers, He made a public spectacle of them, triumphing over them in it. So let no one judge you in food or in drink, or regarding a festival or a new moon or sabbaths, which are a shadow of things to come, but the substance is of Christ." - Col 2: 14**

Simply put, living from the seventh day is living like they did in the Old Testament. However, living from the eighth day is living in a constant feast, it is living from a place of rest, where it is all finished, this life-giving spirit simply dwells in you and flows through you to everything and everyone around you: **"There remains therefore a rest for the people of God. For he who has entered His rest has himself also ceased from his works as God did from His." - Heb 4: 9-10**

and also: **"But he who does the truth comes to the light, that his deeds may be clearly seen, that they have been done in God" – John 3: 21**

The Eighth day is not about a number of things you do right, nor rituals that you keep, nor is it based on performance. The Eighth day has become part of your nature, eternity within you becomes your daily dwelling and reality, it becomes the rivers of life that flow freely from you, the Zoe. You don't force yourself to produce life nor is it dependent on your good works, you just realize [renewing your mind] that the life-giving spirit within you does all the work for you. That is why it says in Revelation that the leaves of the tree are for the healing of the nations and that we have authority over the tree of life.

Please don't let the expression 'authority over the tree of life' confuse you, I am aware that many translations translate this verse to **"they may have the right to the tree of life" yet** if you go back to the original Greek, the word used **in Rev 22:14 is exousia [ἐξουσία]** which means [authority, power, jurisdiction, right, privilege, strength, delegation] you can be content with just having access to the tree of life but let me assure you that what is truly offered to you is way more than just access to the tree of life and eating from its fruit.

The translator did not exaggerate when he chose to use the word "authority" from amongst the various translations and meanings.

This was not just about the mere possibility of access that was offered to us at the beginning of the vision while addressing the Church of Ephesus, saying: **"To him who overcomes I will give to eat from the tree of life, which is in the Paradise of my God". Rev2: 7**

You already have the ability and right to access and eat from the Tree of Life. So why would the Scripture repeat the same thing at the end of the book, after telling us about the new heavens the new earth, and the new Jerusalem descending from heaven!

For the Holy Spirit tells us about our position in Christ saying: **"I am the vine; you are the branches. He who abides in Me, and I in him, bears much fruit; for without Me you can do nothing." - John 15:5**

So, the point is not just access to the tree of life but becoming a branch that bears fruit by abiding in the vine so others through you can have access to its fruit.

This explains what happened with Elisha's bones: **"Then Elisha died, and they buried him. And the raiding bands from Moab invaded the land in the spring of the year. So it was, as they were burying a man, that suddenly they spied a band of raiders; and they put the man in the tomb of Elisha; and when the man was let down and touched the bones of Elisha, he revived and stood on his feet." - 2 Kgs 13: 20-21**

Elisha did not pray for this man to be raised from the dead, he was simply rooted in the living God and was transformed to the likeness of this living God he worshiped so life giving power became part of his nature free flowing from his branch because this branch was simply rooted in the vine.

This also explains to us what Jesus said: **"Then Jesus answered and said to them, "<u>Most assuredly, I say to you, the Son can do nothing of Himself, but what He</u>**

sees the Father do; for whatever He does, the Son also does in like manner. For the Father loves the Son and shows Him all things that He Himself does; and He will show Him greater works than these, that you may marvel. For as the Father raises the dead and gives life to them, even so the Son gives life to whom He will" – John 5: 19-21

"Most assuredly, I say to you, he who hears My word and believes in Him who sent Me has everlasting life, and shall not come into judgment, but has passed from death into life. Most assuredly, I say to you, the hour is coming, and now is, when the dead will hear the voice of the Son of God; and those who hear will live. For as the Father has life in Himself, so He has granted the Son to have life in Himself" – John 5: 24-26

Note that when the Spirit says He gives life to whomever He wills, it reminds me of what the Spirit says about the two witnesses, the two olive trees: **"These have power to shut heaven, so that no rain falls in the days of their prophecy; and they have power over waters to turn them to blood, and to strike the earth with all plagues, as often as they desire." - Rev 11:6**

This is the will of our spiritual man that is attached to the Holy Spirit not the will of the body that lusts against the spirit in order to attract the will of the soul with it.

I and maybe others were taught that the will is found in the soul thus the soul was the only part of us that has a will, but the truth is that each of your soul, spirit, and body has an independent will.

If the will of any two of them are united, it attracts the whole being submitting it to the authority of this will and, accordingly, forms and shapes your mind and the next steps of your path.

Let us stop for a moment, allow these words to renew your mind and bring transformation to your life.

"And do not be conformed to this world, but be transformed by the renewing of your mind, that you may prove what is that good and acceptable and perfect will of God." - Rom 12: 2

For the Lord has opened up and guaranteed a new age: **"Now all these things happened to them as examples, and they were written for our admonition, upon whom the ends of the ages have come" – 1 Cor 10: 11**

For us to pass over from death to life, true life, where we no longer fear death, not physical death but rather what happens after that. Let us begin living eternity here on earth, no need to wait, we can tap into and activate eternity within us and be alive. For without it we won't be able to comprehend the purposes and plans he has for our days here on earth: **"I have seen the God-given task with which the sons of men are to be occupied. He has made everything beautiful in its time. Also, He has put eternity in their hearts, except that no one can find out the work that God does from beginning to end" – Eccl 3: 10-11**

So, with the Lord opening up a new age for us and restoring the authority we had lost due to the fall, it is important that we understand more about this authority and how we are to use it in this new age.

"Then the seventy returned with joy, saying, "Lord, even the demons are subject to us in Your name." And He said to them, "I saw Satan fall like lightning from heaven. Behold, <u>I give you the authority to trample on serpents and scorpions, and over all the power of the enemy</u>, and nothing shall by any means hurt you. Nevertheless, do not rejoice in this, that the spirits are subject to you, but rather rejoice because your names are written in heaven." - Luke 10: 17-20

Yes, you have been given authority to confidently trample on the power of the enemy without the fear of retaliation. So, when Jesus says that the leaves of the tree are for the healing of the nations, he is also saying the curse has been broken.

"And Jesus came and spoke to them, saying, "<u>All authority has been given to Me in heaven and on earth</u>. Go therefore and make disciples of all the nations, baptizing them in the name of the Father and of the Son and of the Holy Spirit, teaching them to observe all things that I have commanded you; and lo, I am with you always, even to the end of the age." Amen." - Matt 28: 18-20

Preaching to the Samaritans was unacceptable before the outpouring of the Holy Spirit on Pentecost, but after, all the nations have a seat at the Lord's table. You have the right to choose between living under the umbrella of the seventh day, bound by following a set of rules as they did in the Old Testament or choose to enter into this new day, this new age of the eighth day where grace and rest ensure that you are no longer enslaved to the fear of death. It is this confidence that gives you the authority to invite others into this day without fearing judgment.

You either live as Solomon described it: **"Then I looked on all the works that my hands had done and on the labor in which I had toiled, and indeed all was vanity and grasping for the wind. There was no profit under the sun." - Eccl 2: 11**

or live according to what was finished and accomplished through the death and resurrection of our Lord Jesus Christ and be seated with him in the heavenly realms above and not under the sun.

"Even when we were dead in trespasses, made us alive together with Christ (by grace you have been saved), and raised us up together, and made us sit together in the heavenly places in Christ Jesus, that in the ages to come He might show the exceeding riches of His grace in His kindness toward us in Christ Jesus. For by grace, you have been saved through faith, and that not of yourselves; it is the gift of God, not of works, lest anyone should boast. For we are His workmanship, created in Christ Jesus for good works, which God prepared beforehand that we should walk in them." - Eph 2: 5-10

Conclusion

To conclude, I would like for us to read a number of verses from the book of John: **"This is the will of the Father who sent Me, that of all He has given Me I should lose nothing but should raise it up at the last day. And this is the will of Him who sent Me, that everyone who sees the Son and believes in Him may have everlasting life; and I will raise him up at the last day" - John 6: 39-40**

"No one can come to Me unless the Father who sent Me draws him; and I will raise him up at the last day" - John 6:44

"Whoever eats My flesh and drinks My blood has eternal life, and I will raise him up at the last day" - John 6:54

Normally in reading these verses we are led to think that Jesus is talking about Judgment. That is not entirely true. If he was talking about judgement, all humanity will be there when everyone will be judged for the choices, they make regardless of what the consequences of these choices are. In these verses Jesus is talking about the new day [the Eighth day] he was about to ordain, otherwise why has he linked it to communion [Jesus is our communion, his flesh and blood]?

If you look closely there is another expression repeated in the verses, which is "the father who sent me" and here he links this day with the great commission given to his disciples being sent out to the world once they had received the Holy Spirit on Pentecost.

This is the purpose of you being sent out into the world, you dwell in a different reality, an ongoing never-ending day of celebration and victory. It is this reality that attracts those around you to Christ and his resurrection power leading them to the eternal life you are already experiencing.

Allow me to conclude by shedding some light on a biblical truth I had pointed out earlier, how a day ends and a new one begins. A new day in the bible begins in the evening, and Paul says: **"The night is far spent; the day is at hand" – Rom 13:12**

and thus, every time you are made aware of the eternal kingdom dwelling inside of you, the closer you get to the **"Light that shines in a dark place, until the day dawns and the morning star rises in your hearts" – 2 Pet 1:19**

until we get to the time when we hear: **"Behold, the tabernacle of God is with men, and He will dwell with them, and they shall be His people. God Himself will be with them and be their God" – Rev 21:3**

How I personally long for that time, where I stand face to face before the father of lights and dwell in this eternal light seeing him as he is, in his fullness. I am not sure how I will react; will I throw myself into his arms or just stand in awe admiring his beauty or will I fall to my knees face down like the angels covered by their wings because of his holiness and the brightness of his glory?

If you are still not convinced despite everything written so far, let us read these verses together: **"Now when the Sabbath was past, Mary Magdalene, Mary the mother of James, and Salome bought spices, that they might come and anoint Him. Very early in the morning, on the first day of the week, they came to the tomb when the sun had risen. And they said among themselves, "Who will roll away the stone from the door of the tomb for us?" But when they looked up, they saw that the stone had been rolled away—for it was very large. And entering the tomb, they saw a young man clothed in a long white robe sitting on the right side; and they were alarmed. But he said to them, "Do not be alarmed. You seek Jesus of Nazareth, who was crucified. He is risen! He is not here. See the place where they laid Him" – Mark 16: 1-6**

I don't think the Holy Spirit used these words "now when the sabbath was past" here just to let us know that the ladies were here to anoint Jesus. I believe he was trying to show us that the sabbath had passed putting an end to the seventh day ushering in a new day. A new age had begun in the last Adam, an age full of rest [not only on a specific day]. Through this rest you are able to bring heaven here on earth, creating gardens of Eden.

You might be asking, what am I supposed to do? How am I supposed to live on the eighth day?

This is how Jesus responds: **"Then they said to Him, "What shall we do, that we may work the works of God?" Jesus answered and said to them, "This is the**

work of God, <u>that you believe in Him whom He sent</u>." - John 6: 28-29

You just have to believe that the Lord prepared a place for you called rest and live from it doing the good works he prepared beforehand for you to walk in. Which will take you back to where it began with Adam, where everything he did from working on the earth, preserving it, and subduing creation was an integral part of his worship, his relationship with God, and his life's call among all of creation.

But his deviation from the divine plan for his life is what brought him out of this rest and is what could also keep you out of this rest too.

The requirement is: renewing your mind to realize the truth of what has been offered up to you in Christ and his new covenant.

I will attempt to bring all the various parts together in case any of you are still questioning which day am I living in?

As we know man is made up of spirit, soul and body, we also know the bible tells us that we are the temple of God made up of the holy of holies, the holy place and the porch.

The temple as we know is ready on the eighth day.

Then there is also the other side of this relationship that is the trinity, Father, Son and Holy Spirit, each represented through the various appointed feasts.

So, during Passover we encounter the redemption of the Son who took on our flesh, our outer porch to purify us and wash us through the water of his word.

He then ascends to send us the comforter, the Holy Spirit whom we feast during Pentecost, to bring us into the Holy place where we find the golden lampstand, representing the seven spirits of God, that enlightens and enflames our spirit but there is also the showbread [the bread of the presence] on the table that satisfies the soul to the extent of us joining the psalmist who wrote: **"You will show me the path of life; In Your presence is fullness of joy At Your right hand are pleasures forevermore" - Ps 16: 11**

Yet unfortunately, we are often so thrilled by the baptism of the Holy Spirit that we neglect the soul, [usually a gateway to our lives that is often used by the enemy], when we tend to try to satisfy it with anything other than the presence of God and become content with just the gifting.

But when we allow the Holy Spirit to freely work on both our spirit and soul together, we will encounter the joy of the final feast in the holy of holies. It is here we find the doorway to the eighth day, opened, when Jesus cried in a loud voice telling us all; "it is finished" tearing open the veil [in the holy of Holies] that kept us from knowing the father, the source of life, the one whom we call the father of lights. Only then we celebrate the feast of the tabernacles.

Remember, in the outer court, the sun and moon are the sources of light, when we move into the Holy Place the golden lampstand lights your path, in the Holy of Holies the only source of light is his presence appearing in the form of a cloud above the mercy seat which is on the arc and within the arc are the two tablets representing the word of God, no wonder the church calls this place the father's embrace.

For in this embrace even the barren rod of Aaron is able to blossom and yield ripe almonds. Here the light of God is at the center of it all and you no longer need to feel lost nor confused.

What Isaiah the prophet said and what the book of revelation tells us is the depth and purpose of what the Holy Spirit is calling us to step into: **"Violence shall no longer be heard in your land, neither wasting nor destruction within your borders; But you shall call your walls Salvation, And your gates Praise. "The sun shall no longer be your light by day, nor for brightness shall the moon give light to you; But the Lord will be to you an everlasting light, And your God your glory. Your sun shall no longer go down, nor shall your moon withdraw itself; For the Lord will be your everlasting light, And the days of your mourning shall be ended. Also, your people shall all be righteous; They shall inherit the land forever, the branch of My planting, the work of My hands, That I**

may be glorified. A little one shall become a thousand and a small one a strong nation. I, the Lord, will hasten it in its time." – Isa 60: 18-22

"But I saw no temple in it, for the Lord God Almighty and the Lamb are its temple. The city had no need of the sun or of the moon to shine in it, for the glory of God illuminated it. The Lamb is its light. And the nations of those who are saved shall walk in its light, and the kings of the earth bring their glory and honor into it. its gates shall not be shut at all by day (there shall be no night there). And they shall bring the glory and the honor of the nations into it." – Rev 21: 22-26

Does this remind you of what the spirit said about the feast of tabernacles?

"You shall dwell in booths for seven days. All who are native Israelites shall dwell in booths, 43 that your generations may know that I made the children of Israel dwell in booths when I brought them out of the land of Egypt: I am the Lord your God." Lev 23:42-43

The Lord didn't mean actual booths but rather the eternal tabernacle of his fatherhood, for as He used to call them while they were still in slavery "the firstborn sons", they are now children surrounding the pillar of cloud by day and the pillar of smoke by night which is their father's presence.

Dwelling in the eighth day is the union of your spirit, soul and body with the fullness of the trinity [Father, Son and Holy Spirit] that is why the writer in the book of Hebrews urges us to enter into this rest for he is fully aware of our nature that tends to be content rather than go deeper.

The Holy Spirit is there to set ablaze both your soul and spirit as well as consecrate you to enter into the father's embrace or Holy of Holies. But our human nature becomes content with just celebrating our baptism in spirit but allow me to shock you: **"Jesus answered, "Most assuredly, I say to you, unless one is born of water and the Spirit, he cannot enter the kingdom of God. That which is born of the flesh is flesh, and that which is born of the Spirit is spirit. Do not marvel that I said to you, 'You must be born again.' The wind blows where it wishes, and you hear the sound of it, but cannot tell where it comes from and where it goes. So is everyone who is born of the Spirit." Nicodemus answered and said to Him, "How can these things be?" Jesus answered and said to him, "Are you the teacher of Israel, and do not know these things? Most assuredly, I say to you, we speak what We know and testify what We have seen, and you do not receive Our witness. If I have told you earthly things and you do not believe, how will you believe if I tell you heavenly things? No one has ascended to heaven but He who came down from heaven, that is, the Son of Man who is in heaven." – John 3: 5- 13**

Isn't it strange for Jesus to describe the baptism of fire to being on the level of "earthly things"?

We tend to focus on anointing, spiritual gifts, signs and wonders, the fulfillment of promises when in truth it should be elsewhere.

The writer of the book of Hebrews urges us to enter into rest. Prayer, fasting and reading the word are all tools to help. It is not our effort in using these tools that makes us enter into rest rather the work of the Holy Spirit in us that helps us train our minds, bodies and souls to never be content with the presence of God and keeps us yearning for more, yearning to know more and explore the depths of God: **"But as it is written: "Eye has not seen, nor ear heard, nor have entered into the heart of man The things which God has prepared for those who love Him." But God has revealed them to us through His Spirit. For the Spirit searches all things, yes, the deep things of God. For what man knows the things of a man except the spirit of the man which is in him? Even so no one knows the things of God except the Spirit of God. Now we have received, not the spirit of the world, but the Spirit who is from God, that we might know the things that have been freely given to us by God." – 1 Cor2: 9-12**

That's what the prodigal son's story tells us, the hope of redemption and the internal voice of the Holy Spirit are what prepare the way back but only the father's embrace makes you a son.

For as the journey of the Lord's feasts leads to the final "feast of tabernacles" also called the feast of the Throne, so does his work of "reconciliation" and the work of the Holy Spirit lead us straight into the father's embrace.

So, the eighth day is the father's embrace.

There HE IS, everlasting light from the greatness of his strength, there all sorrow and sighing flee away.

You can experience the father's embrace once, maybe visit or just be content with information about it, but you can also resist every temptation to make you settle. Listen to what the Bible says about what the ostrich does while confronting the hunter (although she is not wise): **"When she lifts herself on high, she scorns the horse and its rider" - Job 39: 13-18**

For it was never about the spiritual gifts, nor the signs that could move mountains but about the nature of the relationship that is based on love for who He is, nothing else!

Trust me, it is a decision and a choice you constantly make, choosing to believe 'it is finished' and abide in his rest like Jesus did when he slept despite the storm raging all around the boat or trying to live as those of the Old Testament trying to reach this rest depending on their good works and the peaceful circumstances surrounding them.

I invite you to ask the Lord to give you the spirit of wisdom and revelation to know him that you may live out and in fullness all the plans that he has in store for you.

"It is the glory of God to conceal a matter, but the glory of kings is to search out a matter" – Prov 25:2

We have been made kings and priests unto God and his father and I sincerely hope I managed to search out for you the numerous truths concealed in scripture that point to and teach us about the eighth day and who we are when we become aware of this day and choose to abide in it.

If you are certain that you have been made a king and a priest unto God, then you should examine the matter and search out what the book says, because all the books are inspired by the Spirit for the sake of our education, and there is not a letter written in it without a specific goal and an important message for you, and this is what makes me wonder after all these evidences that speak clearly about the eighth day, its importance, and your identity, why some of us still live in the past and leave a better era founded by Jesus with his incarnation, death, and resurrection?

Now put your heart and soul before the Lord, so that He may renew your mind in order to lead you to His eternal dwellings, where He wants.

Blessing, grace and glory to fulfill the divine purpose in your life to the glory of His name.

Amen

www.ingramcontent.com/pod-product-compliance
Lightning Source LLC
LaVergne TN
LVHW090137160826
845673LV00017B/2501

* 9 7 8 9 7 7 3 2 1 3 5 5 8 *